SCHIRMER'S LIBRARY OF MUSICAL CLASSICS

Vol. 341

FRANZ LISZT

Consolations

(Nos. 1-6)

Liebesträume

THREE NOCTURNES

For the Piano

Edited and Fingered by

RAFAEL JOSEFFY

G. SCHIRMER, Inc.

DISTRIBUTED BY

HAL•LEONARD
CORPORATION

7777 W. BLUEMOUND RD. P.O. BOX 13819 MILWAUKEE, WI 53213

Consolations

I

Edited and fingered by
Rafael Joseffy

Franz Liszt
1811-1886

II

Un poco più mosso

III

Lento placido

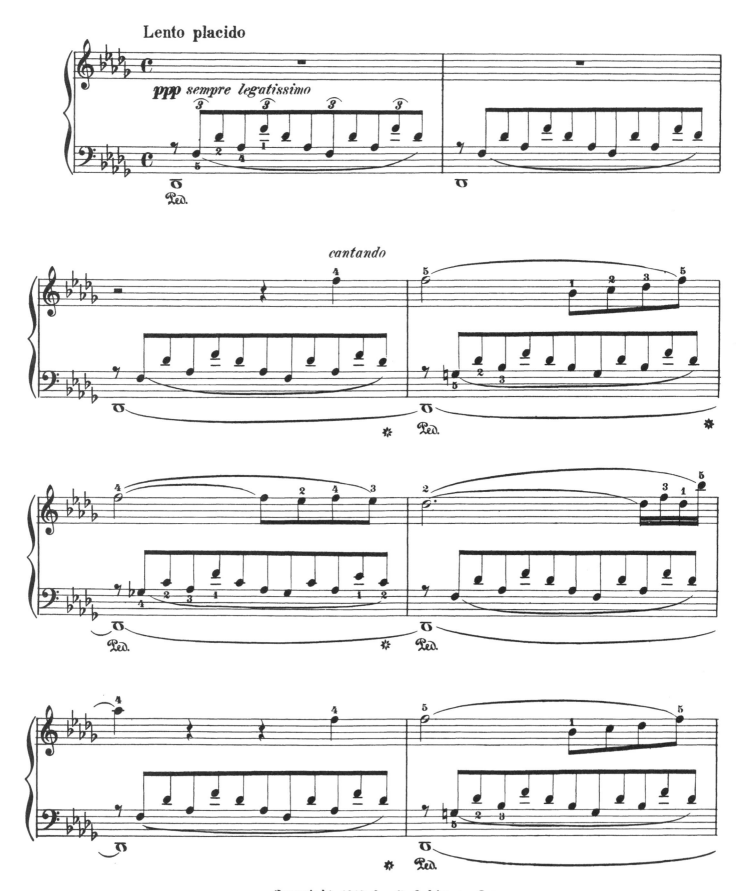

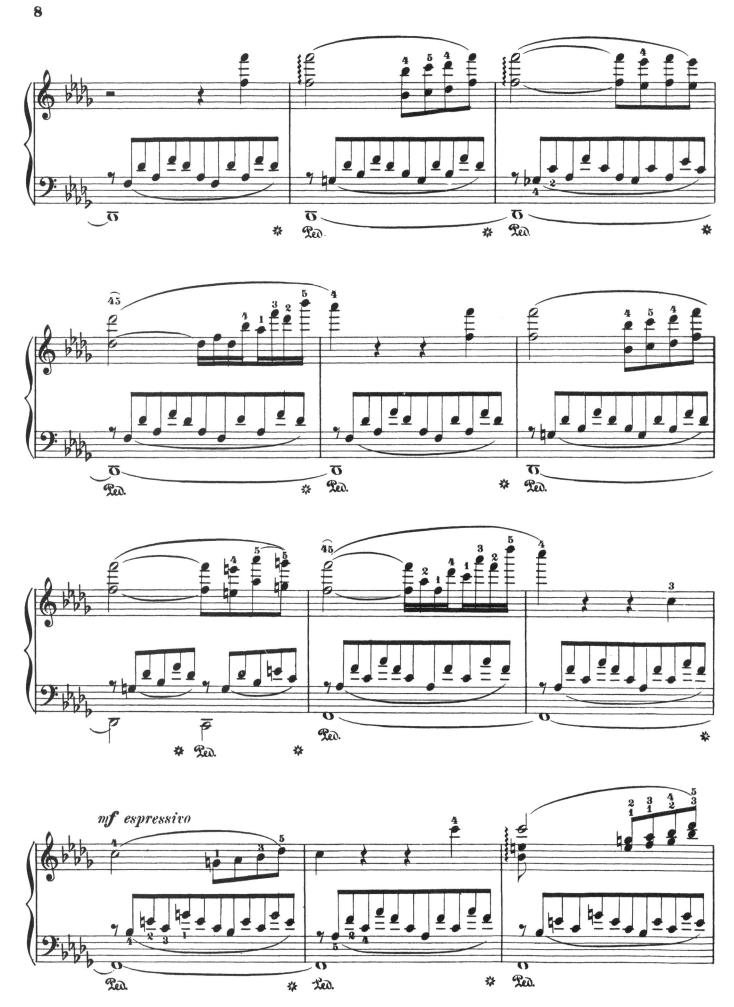

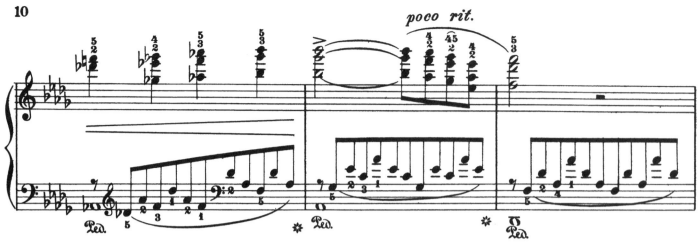

IV

Quasi adagio

cantabile con divozione

13

V

Andantino

con grazia

dolce

16

VI

Allegretto sempre cantabile

appassionato e molto accentato

Liebesträume | Love-Dreams

Notturno I

<table>
<tr><td>

Hohe Liebe
Gedicht von Uhland

In Liebesarmen ruht ihr trunken,
  Des Lebens Früchte winken euch;
Ein Blick nur ist auf mich gesunken,
  Doch bin ich vor euch allen reich.

Das Glück der Erde miss' ich gerne
  Und blick', ein Märtyrer, hinan,
Denn über mir in goldner Ferne
  Hat sich der Himmel aufgethan.

</td><td>

Perfect Love
Poem by Uhland

Within Love's arms to bliss invited
  To ye life's sweet enjoyments call:
On me one glance alone has lighted,
  Yet I am rich beyond you all.

I yield Earth's joys without resistance,
  And, as a martyr, gaze on high,
For over me, in golden distance,
  There opens a celestial sky.

</td></tr>
</table>

Edited and fingered by
Rafael Joseffy

Franz Liszt

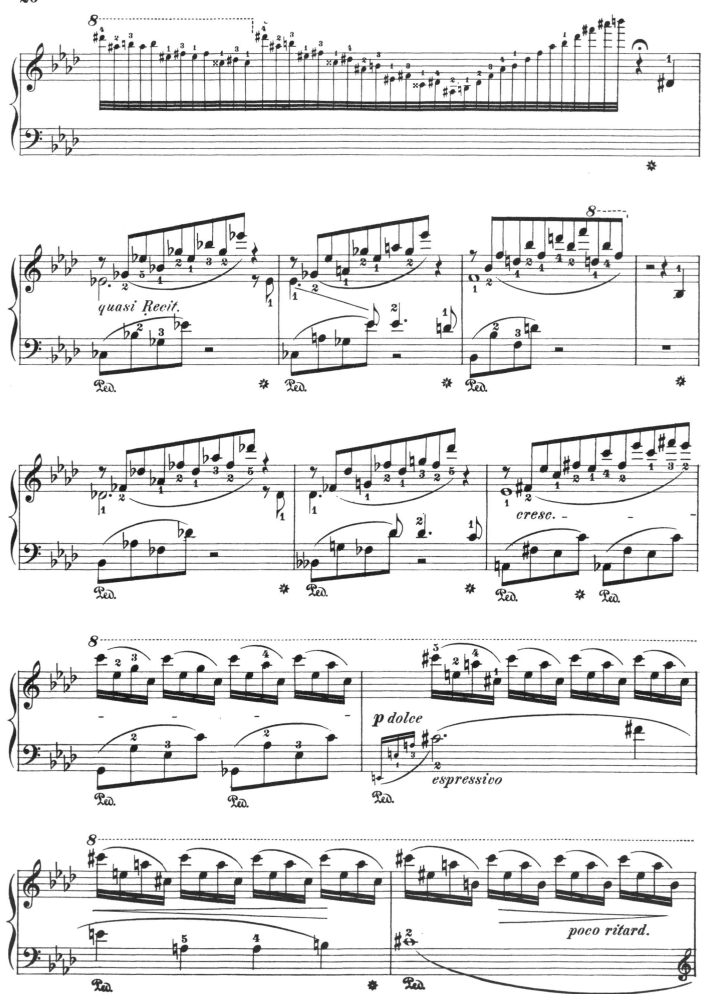

Liebesträume | Love-Dreams

Notturno II

Seliger Tod
Gedicht von Uhland

Gestorben war ich
Vor Liebeswonn',
Begraben lag ich
In ihren Armen;
Erwecket ward ich
Von ihren Küssen,
Den Himmel sah ich
In ihren Augen.

Blissful Death
Poem by Uhland

I was as dead
In love's fond blisses,
And in her arms
Lay buried quite:
I was awakened
By her kisses,
And in her eyes
Saw heav'n's own light.

Edited and fingered by
Rafael Joseffy

Franz Liszt

Quasi lento, abbandonandosi

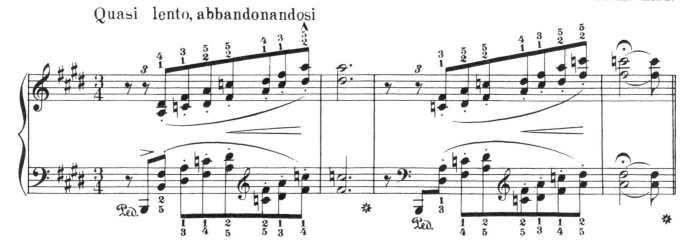

il canto accentato assai

sempre marcato il canto
armonioso

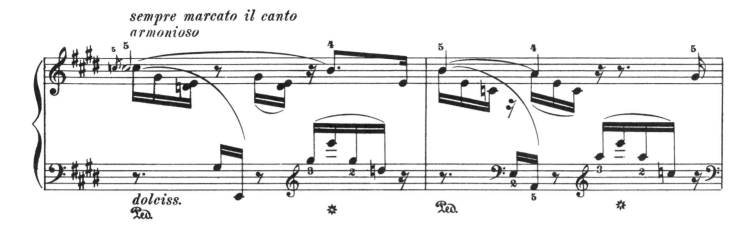

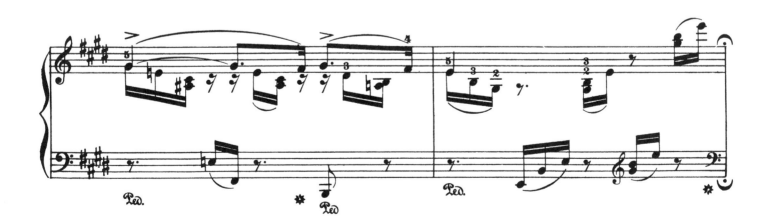

32

Notturno III

„O lieb'"

Gedicht von F. Freiligrath

O lieb', o lieb' so lang du lieben kannst, so lang du lieben magst.
  Die Stunde kommt, wo du an Gräbern stehst und klagst.
Und sorge, dass dein Herze glüht, und Liebe hegt und Liebe trägt,
  So lang ihm noch ein ander Herz in Liebe warm entgegenschlägt.
Und wer dir seine Brust erschliesst, o thu' ihm was du kannst zu lieb,
  Und mach' ihm jede Stunde froh, und mach' ihm keine Stunde trüb!
Und hüte deine Zunge wohl: bald ist ein hartes Wort entfloh'n.
  O Gott— es war nicht bös gemeint—
Der Andre aber geht und weint.

"O love!"

Poem by F. Freiligrath

O love! O love, so long as e'er thou canst, or dost on love believe;
  The time shall come, when thou by graves shalt stand and grieve;
And see that still thy heart doth glow, doth bear and foster love divine,
  So long as e'er another heart shall beat in warm response to thine.
And, whoso bares his heart to thee, O, show him love where in thy power,
  And make his every hour a joy, nor wound his heart at any hour.
And keep a guard upon thy tongue— an unkind word is quickly said:
  Ah me!— no ill was meant— and yet
The other goes and weeps thereat.

Franz Liszt

Poco allegro, con affetto

poco cresc. ed agitato

Più animato, con passione